Meister Eckhart

Rufus Jones

Kessinger Publishing's Rare Reprints

Thousands of Scarce and Hard-to-Find Books on These and other Subjects!

- Americana
- Ancient Mysteries
- Animals
- Anthropology
- Architecture
- Arts
- Astrology
- Bibliographies
- Biographies & Memoirs
- Body, Mind & Spirit
- Business & Investing
- Children & Young Adult
- Collectibles
- Comparative Religions
- Crafts & Hobbies
- Earth Sciences
- Education
- Ephemera
- Fiction
- Folklore
- Geography
- Health & Diet
- History
- Hobbies & Leisure
- Humor
- Illustrated Books
- Language & Culture
- Law
- Life Sciences

- Literature
- Medicine & Pharmacy
- Metaphysical
- Music
- Mystery & Crime
- Mythology
- Natural History
- Outdoor & Nature
- Philosophy
- Poetry
- Political Science
- Science
- Psychiatry & Psychology
- Reference
- Religion & Spiritualism
- Rhetoric
- Sacred Books
- Science Fiction
- Science & Technology
- Self-Help
- Social Sciences
- Symbolism
- Theatre & Drama
- Theology
- Travel & Explorations
- War & Military
- Women
- Yoga
- *Plus Much More!*

**We kindly invite you to view our catalog list at:
http://www.kessinger.net**

III

MEISTER ECKHART

THE fourteenth century in Europe experienced the greatest wave of mystical religion that has ever appeared in any one period of Christian history, and Meister Eckhart is the towering figure in that unique procession of mystical geniuses. It was a period when the century plant of the Spirit bloomed at its richest. Dante, Petrarch, Boccaccio, Chaucer, Cimabue, Giotto, Richard Rolle, Wyclif, Saint Catherine of Sienna and Duns Scotus are a few of the names in that remarkable constellation of great luminaries. They were not all mystics but they were all luminaries. It was a dawning era, heralding a still greater dawn. There seem to be mysterious "mutation" epochs in history when the old levels of life and thought are suddenly passed and when in a burst of surprise a new one is inaugurated. In many aspects the fourteenth century was dark and sad. It had its Black Death, its Babylonish captivity, its imperial and papal schisms, its interdicts, its peasant uprisings and its interminable wars, but it saw also the creation of the greatest Christian poem of all the ages, the erection of the most perfect bell-tower in the world, the culmination of scholastic ingenuity and subtilty, the birth of religious painting, the dawn of the Renaissance and the highest tidal wave of mystical experience.

Why does the poet come at that particular moment, why does the architectural triumph arrive just then, why does the mystic genius flourish precisely at that date? Who can tell when the hour is ripe, who can explain the curve of human progress? The Spirit seems to blow where and when it listeth. There have been a few persons in human history who have felt the life of God with a vividness and a sense of reality beyond what others ever know or feel, and there have also been a few persons who have possessed a unique power of telling about this experience and what it signifies. In the list of the first type I should put Jesus, Saint Paul, Saint John, Saint Augustine, Saint Bernard, Saint Francis, and George Fox. In the second list I should put Plotinus, Dionysius the Areopagite, Saint Augustine, Dante, Eckhart, Ruysbroeck, Jacob Boehme, Saint Teresa, and Saint John of the Cross, while there are many others who belong in one or the other or in both of these lists. Plotinus, though not a Christian, is the "father" of the long succession and it is impossible to conceive of the march of European mystical thought without this Greek prophet at the head of the line.

Eckhart is, I think, the profoundest interpreter of the experience in the long file of those who followed the Alexandrian "father" of the movement. He was not a systematic thinker like Plotinus, and he was not logically as consistent as the Greek philosopher was. But he was much closer in heart to the rank and file of the people. He spoke in the tongue of the common man. He was humble and tender. His fine sympathetic treatment of Martha, the busy burden-bearer, shows his intimate insight into the daily life of those who listened to him. He was, too, always referring with tenderness and gentleness to the purifying and transforming effect of patient suffering, and he ranks it above ecstasy and exalted visions.

It is a thousand pities that we do not have an autobiography from his pen or some letters which tell "how it went with him." It may quite probably be that we could put him in the first list if we knew the facts and experiences of his life. There are intimations, in the *Sermons and Treatises,* that he, like George Fox, had come up through the flaming sword into the paradise of God, had seen and heard and handled, but there are no first-hand accounts of what happened, "when there was mid-sea and the mighty things." We are left to grope in the dark for details of both the outer and the inner life of the man. It was not a century when men wrote autobiographies, though as an exception Suso did, and no disciple had the skill to pass on to us the story of the great mystic's life. We can see him only far off in the mist—a distant peak showing above impenetrable clouds. He is like a massive bowlder which the glacial drift has left. It is not of our rock or strata. It is torn from another age and habitat, but it at least reveals to us the depth and the carrying power of the movement which brought this bowlder into our fields.

I have twice already tried to spell out the lost story of Eckhart's life and to interpret his thought—once in *Studies in Mystical Religion,* and again in a book entitled *At One With the Invisible,* edited by Professor Sneath, but now that we have Eckhart's *Sermons and Treatises* translated both into English and into modern German, there is something more to say. Before this I have always had to dig him out of his own rugged old high German, and it is a satisfaction to be able to read him in contemporary German and comfortable English. But let no one fondly suppose that he can travel through these four hundred and eighty English pages without some gasping and panting.[1] Eckhart is still Eckhart—a mysterious bowlder which the mystical drift of the centuries has deposited. We can walk around him and see his surface, but who can tell what is far within in the central deeps of the man!

Eckhart was studying in the University of Paris when Dante was setting out, "midway in the path of his life," on his marvelous

---

[1] *Meister Eckhart,* by Franz Pfeiffer, translated with some omissions and additions by C. deB. Evans. London, John M. Walkins.

pilgrimage through the realms where the soul of a man awakens to its eternal destiny and finds what kind of a world it has made for itself. Both men owed an enormous intellectual and spiritual debt to Saint Thomas Aquinas, who finished his earthly life (1274) when they were boys, one in Germany, perhaps fourteen at the time, and the other in Florence, then nine years old. Albertus Magnus, Thomas' master, died in 1280, when Eckhart was about twenty, and probably before he came from his home in Thuringia to study in the famous High School of Cologne, where Dominican priests were trained, but the spirit of this scholar, who, like a world conqueror, was named "Magnus," still pervaded the school. Eckhart showed, as so many other great mystics have done, both the traits of Mary and Martha. He was as strong in practical activity as he was in quiet contemplation. A large part of his life was occupied with the complicated work of administration. He was made prior of the Dominican Convent in Erfurt in 1298 and vicar-provincial of Thuringia. His work in the University of Paris began in 1300 and there two years later he received the degree of Master, and by the title of "Meister" he has ever since been known. He was elected provincial of the Province of Saxony in 1303 and re-elected four years later, with the added task of reforming the convents of Bohemia. When his period of service came to an end in 1311 he gave professional lectures in Paris for three years, after which he taught for a short period in Strasbourg. Then came again three years of administrative work as prior in Frankfort, and finally in 1320 he was made professor of the Dominican School at Cologne, where he remained until his death in 1327.

Eckhart knew the fathers and the masters of mystical theology. They appear and reappear by name in his sermons, are reverently cited as authorities, and even when they are not named their influence can everywhere be seen. He shows also the marked influence of the Arabian Commentators of Aristotle, and the tendency of Arabian scholars toward pantheism is in evidence both in his psychology and in his theology.

Let us stop here for a moment and consider the lines of thought and experience which shaped the mental and spiritual life of this great mystical leader of the thirteenth and fourteenth centuries. He was, we must remember, living in pretty much the same intellectual atmosphere which Thomas Aquinas breathed, and he almost completely spanned the period of the lifetime of the great Florentine poet, who also was a mystic of immense depth and range. These men all read the same books and fed their souls on the same spiritual food. Aristotle had, since the middle of the thirteenth century, become the major intellectual influence, working on men's minds as a mighty leaven. But there was another strand of influence which, if less conscious in their thought, was hardly less profound in their lives. This was the neoplatonic line of thought which came down to them through Saint Augustine on the one hand, and on the other through the great mystic who wrote under the name of "Dionysius," and who claimed to be the convert of Saint Paul on the Areopagus in Athens, when the apostle said, "In God we live and move and are."

In what strange ways human torches are lighted by the Spirit! By what unexpected kindly processes the trail of light goes forward across the centuries! A Carthaginian rhetorician, who had been living an unsettled and wayward life, is converted in a garden at Milan and becomes the greatest pillar of the church after Saint Paul, the Christian channel of neoplatonism and the father of Western theology and of Western mysticism. An anonymous Greek scholar, living perhaps in Edessa at the end of the fifth century, turns the system of Plotinus and his followers into an elaborate form of Christian mysticism and transmits it to the gifted minds of the thirteenth and fourteenth centuries.

In the Seventh Book of his *Confessions* Saint Augustine tells us that a Latin translation of certain neoplatonist books—evidently the works of Plotinus—came into his hands in 385 and proved to be one of the most potent influences in preparing the way for his conversion to Christianity. It was here in these books that the young Augustine discovered that the inner eye of the soul is able to see the Eternal Light from which the soul itself has sprung, and he learned for the first time that the Platonists agreed with Saint John in teaching that the Word was with God and that the Word was God. It was again, he says, the books of the Platonists that admonished him to "enter into my inmost self" to find God, and when he sets forth his later attainment of that great goal, it is given in neoplatonic language: "In one trembling flash above the mind I arrived at *That which Is.*" In the sublime experience at Ostia, with his mother by his side, he says, "We came to our own minds, and then passed beyond them . . . with the utmost leap of our hearts. . . . We reached forth and with one flash of thought touched the Eternal Wisdom that abides over all." These famous passages, and that other word of his: "Thou hast made us for thyself, and our hearts are restless until they rest in thee," were to be the guiding light of all later mystics to be formed in the Western Church.

Even more important was the influence of "Dionysius," since he presented, as Saint Augustine did not, a complete and systematized account of the mystic way. He furnished the terms and the vocabulary. He produced in ready-made form the philosophy which became the working basis for all mystics before the Reformation. He accustomed everybody to think of God as absolutely above and beyond all description in terms of qualities and character—a God who is super-everything, and who is to be "known" only through an experience that transcends "knowing." In the middle of the ninth century the Irish scholar, John Scotus Erigena, translated these books of "Dionysius" from Greek to Latin and put them into current thought. They were, of course, given great prestige by the fact that they were believed to be written by the man whom Saint Paul had converted on Mars' Hill who was believed to be the first Bishop of Athens and to be also Saint Denis, the founder of Christianity in Paris, and who finally became, as they supposed, a holy martyr to the faith.

Through these two sources, then, the streams of mystical life and thought flowed into and became a part of European Christianity. Gregory the Great, who was Pope from 590 to 604, and Saint Bernard of Clairvaux (1090-1153), one of the greatest spiritual personalities in the entire history of the church, became powerful transmitters of the mystical inheritance. Saint Bernard gave to it a new note of warmth and passionate love, and he added to mystical literature the glowing and vivid imagery of the *Canticles,* turned into a pictorial drama of the soul wedded to its eternal Bridegroom. The two great Victorines—Hugh and Richard of Saint Victor in Paris—in the twelfth century raised the method of *contemplation* to a place of immense importance, and carried the mystical tradition a new stage forward. In England, Richard Rolle (born c. 1290), one of the earliest English poets, the father of English prose, and a "troubadour of God," was the first great English mystic. Rolle was followed in the middle of the fourteenth century by a great anonymous spiritual genius who translated parts of the writings of "Dionysius" into English and who produced an extraordinary book entitled *A Cloud of Unknowing* which ends with these words of hope: "Not what thou art, nor what thou hast been, seeth God with his merciful eyes, *but what thou wouldst be.*" We may think of Meister Eckhart, then, as the person who gathers up all these streams of mystical life and thought, and who in a very real sense, therefore may be said to be the culmination of neoplatonized Christian mysticism.

Eckhart was a man of books before he became an administrator and a popular preacher, and with all his genius and originality he still carries a large cargo of thought derived from his predecessors and forerunners, which is equally true, of course, of Dante. I often wonder as I am slowly, patiently creeping along through these sermons of Eckhart, what would happen if he could appear among us again and preach his messages to a modern audience! They would be too deep for any congregation that assembles anywhere now—even in our colleges and universities or theological seminaries. It would seem to us food for giraffes, not for lambs, and yet the common people heard him gladly and the multitude crowded in when he preached, as he usually did, in the vernacular speech, and, fortunately, his words were sacredly preserved for coming generations. Mysticism was in the atmosphere then and Eckhart talked in the style and language of his time. We have lost the key both to his phraseology and to the experiences which lay behind his words. We had, however, better not assume too hastily that we have got beyond the stars by which he sailed, or that our modern education has enabled us to reach depths of life and thought unknown to him six hundred years ago.

Two years after Eckhart's death, which occurred, as I have said, in 1327, a papal Bull condemned twenty-eight propositions drawn from his writings. Seventeen of these were pronounced "heretical" and the other eleven were called "ill sounding, rash, and suspect." The Bull declares that "he wished to know more than he should"! There can be no question that "he wished to know" more than the formulated doctrines which the church proclaimed, more than the official authorities could tell him, more than priests or bishops or Popes of the period were able to see. He has his spiritual daughter, "Sister Katrei," say that she cannot find eternal life until she goes on beyond the teaching of the church and beyond the best guidance her confessor can give her and severs all ties with "creatures," that is, human helpers, and puts herself "in the mighty hands of God."

"I am sorry," she says, "that I listened so long to the counsels of men and was deaf to the counsel of the Holy Spirit." This marvelous story of *Sister Katrei* may, I think, be taken as the nearest approach we have to an autobiographical document, and we can, I believe, find revealed in it the steps and stages of the soul's journey upward to God —"the Source from whence the soul flowed forth." But Eckhart was, notwithstanding, a loyal member of the church. He never intended to break with the system that had nurtured him. He had no thought of being a "rebel" or a "heretic." He could hardly have conceived of a great spiritual life going on without the ministration and the means of grace which the church supplied. The nearest he approached to the attitude of the Reformation can be seen in a passage like the following: "As for those who see their salvation in outward practices [what Luther called "works"] I do not say they will be lost, but they will get to God only through hot cleansing fires; for they who do not quit themselves follow not God; keeping hold of themselves they follow their own darkness. God is no more to be found in any bodily exercise than He is to be found in sin. . . . The beginning of the holy life is to be found in the work of the inner man, in vision and in loving."[2]

Eckhart is a true and characteristic "Friend of God" of the fourteenth-century type. He belonged to the church. He loved its sacraments, he accepted its august system, and he was enrolled in its hierarchy, but at the same time he insisted upon the inalienable right of the individual soul to find its own direct pathway to God, and he stoutly maintained that "the school of the Holy Spirit is the highest school of all," in which "a person can learn more in the twinkling of an eye than all the doctors can teach him."[3] "Not all the saints in heaven," he says, "nor all the preaching friars and barefoot monks on earth can stand against one man moved by the truth."[4]

It is among the fragments and sayings of Eckhart that we find the charming story of "a learned doctor" who yearned for some one to instruct him in the way of truth. Finding one day a beggar, his feet all

---

[2] Tractate on *The Kingdom of God.*
[3] *Sister Katrei.*
[4] *Ibid.*

cracked and dirty, his body clothed in rags, he said to the beggar, "God give thee a good day."

"I never had a bad one," said the beggar.

"God give thee good fortune."

The beggar replied, "I never have bad fortune."

"God bless thee."

Said the beggar, "I have never been accursed."

When he is asked what he means by this excessive optimism the beggar explains thus: "Thou dost wish me a good day and I say I never had a bad one. Hungry, I praise God; freezing, I praise God; poor and forsaken withal, I praise God, so I never have a bad day. Thou dost wish me good fortune; I say I never have ill fortune. Whatever God gives or may lay up for me, be it sour or sweet, good or bad, I accept all from God for the best, and so I have no ill hap. Thou dost call down God's blessing upon me. I answer I am not accursed. I have given my will up to God, every whit, so that anything that God wills I will. That is why I am never unblessed."

"Yea," said the doctor, "but suppose God

should choose to cast thee into hell, what wouldst thou say to that?"

"Cast me into hell," said the beggar. "That would spite himself, yet *if* he cast me into hell I should still have two arms to clasp him with. One arm is true humility, and this I should put under him, embracing him all the while with the other arm, which is love. *Better to be in hell with God than in heaven without him.*"[5]

This shows emphatically how far Eckhart and his "Friends of God" have traveled beyond the external and traditional Christianity of their time. Heaven and hell for him, as for Dante, are to be found in the inward state and attitude of the soul. You will be eternally what you are in your deepest inner self. No jugglery will change it; no masses or pilgrimages can alter the eternal moral conditions of life. You must some day meet your naked self, *and it will be what it is*—and that will be heaven or hell. He says boldly: "Theologians speak of hell. I will tell you what hell is. Your state here is your eternal state. This *is* hell or heaven." "Each per-

---

[5] Whittier has attributed this incident to John Tauler of Strasbourg and he has beautifully told it in his poem, "Tauler."

son," he adds, "will be his own judge in this sense, namely, that the state he then appears in [at death] he will be in eternally."[6]

Eckhart, like all great prophets of the spiritual life, is forever done with schemes of barter and double-entry bookkeeping. His "Sister Katrei" says: "Though there were neither hell nor heaven, I would follow God for true love all the same. I would follow him to the end, without a 'why' [that is, without calculation], or other reason than himself." He goes the whole way out on the road where the milestones are not counted. *Love*, for him, must be washed clean of all self-seeking, of all thought of a return. "To be able to say, 'I love thee, Lord,' a person must suffer without why that which without why Christ suffered, and he must suffer it joyously and gladly. Though God should tell him mouth to mouth, 'Thou shalt be lost forever with the damned,' he only loves God all the more, and says, 'Lord, as thou wilt that I be damned, damned I will be eternally.' That person can truly say to God, 'I love thee.'" It is a relief to our modern minds that Eckhart was absolutely sure to

[6] *Sister Katrei.*

begin with that God could not, from his very moral nature, damn a soul that did not deserve to be damned; for, after all, hell consists only in being *eternally what you are.*

"Art thou looking for God," he asks in the Sermon numbered XI, "seeking God with a view to thy own personal good, thy personal profit? Then in truth thou art not seeking *God.*" He cites a philosopher who says, "He who has once been touched by truth, by righteousness, by goodness, though it entailed the pangs of hell, that man could never turn therefrom, not for an instant," and he adds his own conclusion: "The man who is moved by truth, righteousness, and goodness can no more quit these three things than God can quit his Godhead." In his fortieth Sermon he declares: "If thou seekest aught of thine own, thou wilt never find God, for thou art not seeking God merely. Thou art seeking something with God, making a candle of God, as it were, with which to find something, and then having found it, throwing the candle away." There are plenty of persons, he says in another Sermon, the twelfth, "who follow our Lord half way, but not the other half." Eckhart's peculiarity consisted in going "the whole way" to the very end.

There is a story out of this same fourteenth century which tells how an old woman was seen one day in the streets of Strasbourg carrying a torch in one hand and a bucket of water in the other. When she was asked what her strange performance signified, she said that with the torch she was going to burn up heaven and with the bucket of water she was going to put out hell fire, so that henceforth men could be good for the mere love of God and of goodness and not for the sake of results in the unseen world. She had no doubt heard Eckhart preach and was giving a vivid pictorial illustration of his frequent theme.

The central note in Eckhart's Sermons, and his most important contribution to mystical thought, is his profound interpretation of the nature of the soul. "God made man's soul so like himself," he says in the sixth Sermon, "that nothing else in heaven or earth resembles God so closely as does the human soul." "To measure the soul," he says in his *Sister Katrei,* "you must gauge it with God, for the ground of God and the ground of the soul are one nature." "When I saw into myself," he says in the same tractate, "I saw God in me and everything God ever made in earth and heaven." The truth is to be found not outside, it is within, wholly within. "Ye men, why do ye look without for that which is within you?"

But the truth is not in the surface-mind; it is deep down in the ground and innermost center of the soul, as subsoil wealth. This innermost core of our being Eckhart calls by many different names, such as "Fünklein" or "Spark," "Apex of the Soul," "Centre," "Ground," "Synteresis," "Innermost Essence," "Inner Light," "Bottomless Abyss," "The Arcanum of the Mind"; but however he names it, he is always maintaining that there is something in the soul that is unsundered from God and that indivisibly attaches to the divine nature. This exalted doctrine of the soul is, of course, not new with Eckhart. His forerunners had already held that man's soul is not from the realm of matter nor from the world of space. It is at its highest point of the same nature as God. Aristotle taught that the active creative reason in man can have no earthly origin, while Plotinus went even further and talked of mind and soul as emanations of God, but they are emanations that in going out never actually *leave* their source, as our ideas are still ours however much we utter them. There is an apex or center within us that can never let go and break away from its divine life and spiritual fount. It is because Eckhart believes that there is a junction of the soul with God in the inner deeps of the soul that he can so emphatically declare that "nothing is so close to us as God."

"God is nearer to me than I am to myself."[7] "Thou need not seek Him here or there, He is no further off than the door of thy heart."[8] "In her superior powers the soul is in contact with God."[9] "No man ever wanted anything so much as God wants to make man's soul aware of Himself. God is always ready, but we are far from Him. God is in, we are out; God is at home, we are away somewhere."[10] "When the soul enters into her Ground, into the innermost center of her being, divine power suddenly

---

[7] Sermon LXIX, C. deB. Evans, p. 171.
[8] Sermon IV.
[9] Sermon LII.
[10] Sermon LXIX.

pours into her."[11] "In the Spark, or center of the soul, there occurs true union between the soul and God."[12] "When I saw into myself I saw God in me."[13] "If the soul knew herself, she would know all things."[14] "Where God is there is the soul, and where the soul is there is God."[15]

These random quotations from Eckhart are sufficient to show how bold and daring this fourteenth-century preacher could be. There is something in us, he insists, which has never left its fontal Source and Origin. Travel as far as we may into the world of change and mutability, what he calls "this coil of nether things," we nevertheless remain always at one point in contact with the eternal being of God. There is something which does not let go of him or sever from him, in all the surgings, the ebbs and flows of our temporal life. It is as though in all the mazes of our earthly wanderings we always have hold of an Ariadne thread which connects us with our Guide, a thread that quivers and pulls with all the life and love of God. We are, at the center or Apex of

---

[11] Sermon LXXI.
[12] Sermon LXXIX.
[13] *Sister Katrei.*
[14] Sermon X.
[15] Sermon LXXXIII.

our soul, joined in essence with him, as spirit with Spirit.

"Why do ye ever go out?" he cries. "Why not stop at home and mind your own treasure? For indeed the whole truth is native in you."[16] It is always possible to withdraw from temporal things, from our busy activities and hot pursuits, and to *center down* into this unlost divine inheritance within us. We are suddenly *at home*. We have entered That which Is—the changeless and eternal. We have come upon the primal Source. We are beyond the distinctions of time and place, healed of the wounds that come from our private preferences, by the plunge into the living unity of the Godhead. The floodgate which takes us into the silent refuge where God repairs these broken vessels of ours is close at hand within our own selves.

It is, however, not enough to sink down into the deeps of the soul, to leave the noises of the world behind, and to enter into the stillness of the Godhead. Man's supreme business here on earth is to let God give birth to his own nature in the soul, or, as Eckhart

---

[16] Sermon XIII.

usually puts it, to let God bring forth his Son in the soul. God in his deepest nature as the Ground and Source of all reality is called by Eckhart the Godhead. As naked Godhead he is utterly beyond our comprehension. But as he comes forth out of his hidden and ineffable being into revelation and expression he is then God made manifest. The most perfect manifestation of God is to be seen in Christ, who is by nature what God himself is. But not once only does God bring forth his Son. Every soul is susceptible to this birth of God, and God strives in every one of his human creatures to accomplish this marvelous event. "The best thing God ever did for man," Eckhart says, "was to become man himself," and the highest moment in any man's life is that moment when the divine nature as a spiritual seed becomes the active, dominating principle in the man. Then the "old man" is transformed into a "new man." This is for Eckhart a mystical event of the highest order. When God has brought forth his Son in a man there arises in the soul a love-spring, a joy like the joy of birds. There is a welling-in of life and power. There is a burst of exuberant spirit. Not only the deep ground of the soul now partakes of God and shares in his being, but the whole human nature of the man is shot through with the light and love of God—the man becomes by grace what Christ was by nature. God is essentially spiritualized being, and when God brings forth his Son in us we too by his life in us become at length spiritual beings in our new-found nature.

The most baffling thing to deal with among the problems of life and thought is the real meaning of *time* and *space*. Do they belong to the ultimate nature of the universe or are they caused by our manner of perceiving? Are they truly real or are they only specious? Are they facts of reality or are they facts only of appearance? Do they pertain to the deepest essence of things or only to the surface accidents? Eckhart's answer is closely allied to the ancient Platonic one —he calls Plato "that great priest who occupied himself with lofty matters." He holds space and time to belong only to the world that is cast as a shadow of the real one—the world of appearance which is like a reflected image in a mirror. "If my face were eternal," he says in Sermon XXXIX, "and were held before a mirror, the face would be received in the mirror as a temporal thing, albeit eternal in itself." "God," he says in the eleventh Sermon, "is *truth, but things in time are not truth.*" It is so with everything that appears to our senses —an eternal reality is splashed out into space and time, and so changed to "appearance." All that is real and true for Eckhart is time-free and space-free. It is not in process; it Is. It does not change; it Abides. It has no before and after; it is an eternal Now. He is adhering to a very ancient and honorable system of thought. He is merely reaffirming the well-known tradition that what is perfect cannot change into something else, for then it would become either more perfect or less perfect; consequently he sees no way to insure perfection except to think of it as belonging in a sphere above our kind of world where events proceed from before to after.

Any description of his "eternal Now" is bound to be marked with inconsistency, because we men with our time goggles on are always prone to think of this "eternal Now" as *an infinitely long stretch* in which "nothing happens"—an endless quiescence. That is entirely to miss Eckhart's meaning. What he is endeavoring to say is that all that is true and real, beautiful and good in the entire universe is held together in an undivided unity as one living whole, somewhat as a musician holds the multitudinous notes of his symphony in one unbroken melody which transcends the successive time-notes. Eckhart's moments of mystical experience seem to bring him into a state so exalted and so completely time-free that he interprets the whole life of God in terms of it—a moment like *that* seems to him to have the richness of "an eternal Now."

God and the soul are, in Eckhart's way of thinking, not in space or time—they belong to what is intrinsically, or essentially, *real*. "If," he says, "the soul were stripped of all her sheaths, God would be discovered all naked to her view and would give himself to her, withholding nothing. As long as the soul has not thrown off all her veils, however thin, she is unable to see God."[17] The Apex of the soul, the *Fünklein,* is a timeless, an

---

[17] Sermon XLII.

eternal reality. "At its summit the soul has no connection with time."[18] "There is one loftiest part of the soul," he says, "which stands above time and knows nothing of time or of body," that is, of things in space.[19] "At the summit of the soul time has never entered and no form was ever seen at the summit of the soul."[20] Again he says, "There is a power in the soul untouched by time and flesh, flowing from the Spirit, remaining in the Spirit, altogether spiritual. In this power is God, ever verdant, flowering in all the joy and glory of the actual self."[21] When we "rise past our own mind to the summit of mind," from this divine eminence we have "an inkling of the perfection and stability of eternity, for there is neither time nor space, neither before nor after, but everything present in one new fresh-springing *now,* where millenniums last no longer than the twinkling of an eye!"[22] "I have often said," he declares, "that God is creating the whole world now this instant."[23] Eternity is not something before time began or after time shall be over. Eternity is *a timeless now,* in which God and

---

[18] Sermon XCV.
[19] Sermon XI.
[20] Sermon LXVI.

[21] Sermon VIII.
[22] Sermon XII.
[23] Sermon LXVI.

the soul have no need for clocks or calendars, nor for rapid transit from place to place. "Time ends," says Eckhart, "where there is no before and after."[24]   Everything that *is* is now and here for the spirit that partakes of God, for the soul in whom the divine birth has occurred.

> "Alles vergängliche
> Ist nur ein Gleichniss,"

Goethe wrote at the end of *Faust*. "Everything transitory is only a symbol or parable." That is what the Platonists and their disciples, the mediæval mystics, are always saying. The real world is not in space and time—it is a super-temporal, a super-spatial reality. The trouble with this exalted view is that it at once makes everything real and eternal absolutely unknowable for us who live in time and a *sheer blank* for our human observation and thought. Eckhart, of course, knows that as well as any critic does —he knows it and he glories in it. God, that is, the God-head, the ultimately Real, for him is "the nameless Nothing," "the empty Desert where no one is at home."

---

[24] Sermon **XCIV**.

God, he says, and likewise the soul born of God, is "beyond time, in eternity above images," "above multiplicity." He is "essence," not "accident"—"pure unadulterated being." We cannot know what God is; "we can only know what he is not." "The mind must be raised to an *unknowing knowing*." "Where creature stops, God begins." "Enter God, exit creatures." "To know God is to know him as unknowable."

These are surely hard sayings. They are not only "hard" for the simple lowly lambs; they are "hard" also for the giraffes with their high heads. Something is wrong when the solution of a problem is more difficult to understand than the problem itself! We have left our type of rationality behind when we begin to talk of "unknowing knowing," and when we relegate the supreme reality of our universe to the blank of "a nameless Nothing," to "the empty stillness of absolute Naught." This is only another way of saying that the problem of life, of thought, of religion, like the problem of the relation between the circumference and diameter of a circle, is insoluble in terms of our mind, and that our best gesture under the circumstances

is to put the hand upon the mouth! If space
and time are unreal, and everything the mind
can deal with is only "appearance," and if
God and the essence of the soul belong to
an order of being to which space and time
do not in any sense attach, then, of course,
Eckhart is right and about both these supreme realities we can say nothing, know
nothing, think nothing. We must, as he
says, "turn to *unknowing* to find them."

I am, however, not ready yet for his alter-
native. It lands him in the deepest, dark-
est agnosticism and nescience. It writes
"mene" on the whole visible frame of things.
Evermore we come out by the same door as
in we went. We arrive nowhere. It makes
the incarnation an unreality. It nullifies the
significance of moral struggle. It turns evo-
lution and historical progress into an empty
dream. It lands us in a chaos of *maya* and
illusion. There is nothing stable for our feet
to stand upon. The Holy Grail itself becomes dust and ashes. Eckhart consistently
turns the gospel story into a subtle allegory.
Everything Christ said and did stands in his
mind for some remote and hidden reality.
The miracles and parables point to timeless

truth. When we turn to Eckhart's sermon on the son of the widow of Nain, we find that the widow stands for the soul. Her son represents the intellect, and we are whirled away from the event at Nain to something beyond space and time. Nothing is what it obviously and naturally *seems* to be. Eckhart is doing no more than any other scholar of his time in his farfetched use of allegory. It was an obsession all the way down from Philo to the Reformation, and it blinded all eyes to the simple glory and beauty and truth of the gospel story.

But it is impossible legitimately to pass by allegory from a world where events happen, a world of joy and sorrow, a world of moral and spiritual issues, to a world where time and space, before and after, have ceased to exist. We are left gazing at a blank. We change our rich, colorful world for a pure abstraction. Our human vocabulary loses all its meaning. We are in very truth in "a desert where no one is at home." Nothing in this world of ours is a bit like that world of infinite immobility and absolute immutability. Our figures all fail, our allegories all miss the mark, our similes are futile. There is a chasm between the two worlds which nothing can bridge, not even imagination. Nothing we know, or can know, under this system of thought throws the least light upon the nature of the world yonder. God as he is revealed to us in time and space is wholly unlike the Godhead who remains for us hidden, changeless, unknowable, of whom we can only say: "Not! Not! Not this! Not that! Not here! Not there!" There is no hope in Christianity, nor in any form of religious faith, if we must go to the needy world of our time and say to men who are in quest of light and relief that God is an unknown timeless Center of quiescence, shut up in the tranquillity of his own inner being, never to be known or found here in our vale of mutability, where birth and death, and love and hate, smiling and weeping are real events for us.

Eckhart is not to blame for this impasse. It was not quite so sharply put by his forerunners. But he found it and he left it. He went round and round this sheer rock which no man had ever climbed, and he left it standing there in "a mist of unknowing." This "negative" philosophy is no proper or inherent part of mysticism. It belongs to a long and tragic stage of human thinking. I do not want to do anything to perpetuate it. I want to transcend its abstract reality by substituting for it a reality that is self-communicative and concrete. Instead of being a God whose glory consists in hiding himself in solitary detachment in the desert where nothing stirs, God finds himself in the stress and strain of world-building, in the web and tissue of the moral and spiritual victories of history, of art and of religion, in the slow tragic redemptive work of the ages. He is of such a nature that he can be truly revealed in the events of space and time and history. He is a being, not of abstractness and negations, but of character and purpose.

He is not unknown and unknowable—an inscrutable X—but a God who can make his character known in the love and friendship and sacrifice of Christ, and in our own loyalties and fellowships and moral strivings —a Spirit living in and working with our finite human spirits. To find him we are not compelled to resort to an ecstatic flight into a state in which all the conditions of human existence cease to operate, and from which we can bring back no garnered fruit for use in our hard temporal present. We can find him as a vital healing Presence in the hush and quiet within the deeps of our own souls, and we can find him too wherever we valiantly take up the tasks and duties which spring out of our corporate human relationships. If we are to maintain a triumphant mystical faith to-day, it must fit some such philosophical outlook as that. What Milton said about "cloistered virtue," I should say about a hidden, retired, withdrawn and abstract God: "I cannot praise a fugitive and cloistered virtue, unexercised and unbreathed, that never sallies out and sees her adversary, but slinks out of the race, where that immortal garland is to be run for, not without dust and heat!"

Time and space are, I believe, not unreal. They are not dim shadows of appearance. They are not reflections in a mirror. They have their basis of truth and reality in the essential nature of a spiritual universe. Instead of endeavoring to eliminate them as something foreign and defeative, we need, rather, to rise through them to those experiences and insights of unity and wholeness in which we see the meaning of the process and the significance of the struggle in a time-span which holds past, present and future together in a significant *now*. Perhaps God's time-span is an eternal Now in which the entire world-process has its meaning revealed and its justification affirmed. What a moment that would be!

If I cannot indorse and praise Eckhart's abstract and negative philosophy, I can, nevertheless, greatly commend his beautiful spirit and his effective practical faith which towered above his theoretic philosophy and triumphed in spite of his agnostic creed. He had struggled manfully with the most baffling questions of life, he was utterly free from hypocrisy and completely honest with all men and with himself, and without knowing how he did it, he somehow scaled the rock and found himself "close upon the shining tablelands to which our God himself is moon and sun." His contemporaries said that "God hid nothing from Meister Eckhart," and I feel as I read his Sermons, stocked though they are with bad philosophy and worse allegory, that something divine and holy keeps breaking through them. His hearers did not altogether understand him, but they felt an unusual spiritual energy and power coming through *his God-receptive* life. He knew the might of humility and meekness. "Even God," he says, "cannot thwart the humble soul that has towering aspiration." "I would stake my life," he says, "upon the fact that by strength of will a man can pierce a wall of steel."

He is a rare interpreter of love and it is not love in the abstract—it is love that proves itself by loving. Take this fine sentence: "What I thank God most for is for not being able of his greatness to leave off loving me."[25] That broke out of his own deep experience and it makes us know that for him the love of God is no abstraction above space and time, but a warm and tender fact of life. "I have said many times and say again," he declares in his twenty-eighth Sermon, "that *everything our Lord has ever done he did simply to the end that God might be with us and that we might be one with him, and that is the reason why God was made man.*" "The best thing God ever did for man," as I have already quoted, "was to become man

---

[25] Sermon LXXIII.

himself." With all his emphasis on "detachment," "contemplation," withdrawal from the outside to the inside, he nevertheless declares that "it is better to feed the hungry than to spend one's time in contemplation."[26] And he has much to say in favor of busy Martha, who provides the food necessary for life. Again and again he quotes Saint Augustine's phrase, *"The soul is where it loves."* It is the love-spring arising in the soul which bears it back to God.[27]

With love comes suffering, and Eckhart is an expert in the meaning of suffering. In one of his most noted sayings he declares, "A life of rest and peace in God is good; a life of pain in patience is still better; but to have peace in the midst of a life of pain is best of all."[28] "Nothing," he says in his great sermon on suffering, the hundred and fourth, "makes a man so like God as suffering." "I say that next to God there is no nobler thing than suffering. . . . If anything were nobler than suffering, God would have saved mankind therewith."

Our theories and speculations are frail

[26] Sermon CI.
[27] Second Tractate.
[28] Sermon LXIX.

and transitory. They cost much sweat and blood and they are precious to *us* as the off-spring of our brain, but the heart reaches further and its fruit is much more permanent. When all the chaff of mediæval speculation is winnowed away from these sermons of the great Dominican preacher, the inner spiritual kernel remains as sound and nourishing as when the people crowded in to hear his bold words in their own tongue.

This is the end of this publication.

Any remaining blank pages are for our book binding
requirements and are blank on purpose.

To search thousands of interesting publications like this one,
please remember to visit our website at:

http://www.kessinger.net

Printed in the United States
92630LV00005B/174/A